dystHOPEia

A LAST TESTIMONY FROM FALLEN EARTH

dystHOPEia

Paperback ISBN: 978-1-915223-36-4

Published by

Maurice Wylie Media
Your Inspirational & Christian Book Publisher

For more information visit
www.MauriceWylieMedia.com

Dedication

To those who, across the years
by God's grace alone, directed their gifting
toward the diminishment and destruction
of satan's kingdom.

Contents

Part 1

Down the deep cavern

"For all have sinned
and fall short of the glory of God."

(Rom 3:23.)

DOWN THE DEEP CAVERN

Down the deep cavern
venom unleashed,
poisoned fruit clamour,
wails of deceit,
underground and over
midst world's decay,
demonic dungeons
announce far reach hate.

Witness the living,
the innocent and damned,
for each a short time span
afore life's final demand,
few shepherded to the right,
others appointed the left,
narrow path to life,
a wide canyon heralds death.

In this soon to be over
all wait shrouded in mire,
dead in countless lies,
readied for lime soak pyre,
your Master will soon thee beckon
at hour thou dost not know,
down the deep cavern,
hope only to those
who in this life repent.

This is a tale of what awaits
beyond the grasp of earth's prison bound gate.

Through cursed soil,
thistle soak ditch sink
and brackish mud sludge thick,
through vale, dale and dust track beat,
thorn hedge and briar stick neat,
darkened trees
limb twist stretch,
farm a fallow;
ploughed slick.
Through wind that bellows,
hail and sleet,
blinding sun scorch
to poison rain seep,
a sweeping sin stench
through clock time mist.
From quiet shire lane
to far cobble
rock worn street,
all lies in rust
wholly incomplete,
all corrupt,
the strong and weak.

Come venture this cavern dug deep,
while all rest,
all asleep,
peasants, connivers,
the rich, the poor,
captains of industry in Babel topped towers,
leaders, creepers, young and old,
rulers, monarchs and those far from such power,
all corrupt,
the living, the dead,
in this bleak horizon of cloud drench wet.

Come observe the folly of men,
who run their race then try begin again.
This expanse of history,
full disclose of time;
all corrupt,
all to die...

Decaying entropy advanced slowly through time
at generations pace to keep the populations blind,
while all around a merry fellow dance,
drinking and marrying, masked in a trance,
stand back, slow...begin your review,
a steady creep tentacle, all morals askew,
values eroded by agendas through law
with scant regard replacing old with new.
Hail Fellow Merry,
his no thoughts programmed by design,
engineered craftily with reason and rhyme,
earth's only interest it seemed to remain;
pursuit of pleasure
fortified amply by bread and by games.

Observe alliance,
unholy trinity,
the black arts of sorcery's science,
mixing its business with the potency of religion and politics,
imperfect marriage this union of cruel,
infiltrated these carcases each nation and town,
spawning division in family by home.
With blaring echo of newscast storm
emerged fear spread by realm's coin:
with manipulated intent
they battered the lost,
no matter what spent,
no matter the cost,
deceptions delusion merged no truths,

unconscious assimilation by elders and youth.
Overground this hybrid spread,
injecting the innocent with their poison of death.
Plotters met at their compassed Lodge,
caroused red blush in their palaces and halls,
constructing their laws remaining detached in their thrones.
Secret oaths swopped in blood washed deceit,
covens and cauldrons and black witch stink,
those involved given thrice to satan,
reserved soon for judgement;
destination the pit.

Masons, witches and hood caped wizards,
cloven feet, pointed tailed lizards,
to their doom,
their shame,
they massacred the innocent,
drawing young blood to bathe and to drink.
Skullsluggers
in satanic fellowship,
plotting premeditated murder;
crimson stained, contentions defile.
To their own deaths they ran
these Molech sworn heathen,
pagan spirits in demonic disguise.
Unclean rituals,
blinded,
lost,
faces for flame with furnace hot poke,
skulls and cross bones,
hidden handshakes,
signets, symbols, crooked smiled treason,
hoodwinked, robed, devoid of all reason,
political manoeuvrings in open plain sight,
clamouring quickly toward each their own end;
this atmosphere's baphomets will slow roast in hell.

Churches too,
rotten,
wide hand hewn steeples,
teaching vainly the traditions of men,
dragging confused searching people likewise to hell.
Black clad crows,
collars deceiving, tombwashed white,
devilish defilers of children
stealthily seducing widow's last mite.
Sacrificed they too their idol gods made from bread
pulling Christ Jesus from heaven to murder Him again.
By works of their laws
they terminated grace,
Yahweh's Son's gift that facilitated repent,
liberty exchanged for controlling rod,
priestly dispensation from bribe bought nod.
They hid behind chalices,
laced knots embroidered in golden thread,
selling salvation for ransom;
inventing purgatory's release for the dead.
Purveyors of evil,
plying doctrines of fraud,
politicking with presidents,
this world's kings accustomed to ambassadorial laud,
shrouded in royal purple,
feasting merrily on fat,
deposed they the truth bearers
and deflected God's light.
We are the way, the truth, the life,
heaven secured by our very hands,
Cain's works held high so each acolyte can boast.
Kissers of medallions and statues of stone,
braying voices of forked tongue hurl,
screaming their lies till all subjugated have heard.

Scientists transact in trinity three,
conjuring spells potions in shiny bright vials,
measuring formulas, dispensing lies,
offering opinions while the patient dies.
Antidepressants prescribed with haste and ease,
chemical solutions for life's malaise,
opioids, painkillers popped like sweets,
concoctions brewed for every disease,
loops to jump in this whole foray,
cures available if the fees you can pay.
Insurance won't cover the recipient's expense,
while parliament will not this plight soon address.
Pharmacovigilance, adverse events;
won't document all for the number is great.
Exploring graphene toxins for God's image bearers to ingest
while doctors and sorcerers peddle scripts.
Gain of function research, testing tools,
advantageous results expounded while Mengele rules.

But what is wrong you say?
These corporations cure disease!
But each does work so cruel, not revealed,
splicing and sequencing to fabricate new forms of life,
birthing mixed seed chimera,
distorting all humankind,
condemning that which is sacred,
leaving all that is ethical and wholesome behind.
Science's next step will try to roboticize mankind,
an evolutionary shuffle march
while Hail Fellow Merry remaining silent, turns blind.

These monsters,
villains three,
reduced people to a money grab,
socially engineering the peasants,
enslaving branded worker bees to service debt;

mortgaging lifestyles to obfuscate thinking,
bonded forever,
unable to act.
This unholy hybrid of satan,
manipulated they a canny web.

Participant potentates forsook and abandoned first calling,
turned their very souls from light to decay,
leaders forgot their considered manifestos,
religions turned to worship rough chiselled stone,
conglomerates spurned Hippocratic promises,
all corrupt,
all chose gold...

Overland roam demons wild,
one third the angelic realm,
legions,
created for glory,
took upon a darkened frame,
transfixed by earth's daughters
birthed forth their hideous design.
Satan desires man's worship,
his time though be soon cut short,
Gadarene spirits will drown in swine,
will plunge to the depths of hell's molten crust.
Eden's scourge will pick his name,
someone to implement evil's Jezebel spirit,
tempter's fingerprints directed every page,
Nimrod, Pharaoh and Nebuchadnezzar.
Herod too despatched his fair share,
all sifted like Judas Iscariot.
Recent century's spawned their antichrists,
murdering each generation their droves,
technology now advances blood's sacrifice carnage,
hastening misery by bomb-blast
and delivering tempest by drone.

Satan has distracted, bitten at heal,
will lie crushed at the end,
his demise to be inflicted by heavens wrought zeal.

Isis, Horus, Semiramis,
an ogre army of hosts,
Tammuz, a dead son; they pretended he rose,
Baals and Ashtoreths over time all judged,
Molech demanding children,
Dagon and Chemosh hand sculpted in dust.
Mythologies and legends claimed their allegiance,
destroyed they the peoples in nations of old,
Egyptian gods, Assyrian, Babylonian statue contrivances,
deposed forever but in Machiavellian minds still glow.
Each nation of earth favours their deity,
most constructed to images of stone,
laboured the peoples all to their Baals,
golden claves worshiped,
shaking of bones.
Cultures, traditions blended by season,
superstitions ignite demoniac's playground,
portals opened,
obfuscating all reason,
the walking dead transformed to blue corpses of cold.

Terrors by night,
pestilences dark walking,
noonday destruction
baying for blood,
satan's jigsaw piecing many complications,
difficult to discern the lies from the truth.
Hail Fellow Merry,
nourished drunk on poisoned root,
the wicked in harmony,
trampling,
all good squashed brutally underfoot.

From underground corruption roars,
Abaddon beast of cavern's cage,
deep in earth's subterranean crypt,
a demonic host await in chains.
Millennia they've waited,
fury unkempt, blacksmith forged,
wrath's retribution slowly born,
awaiting their mission from their darkened abode.
Grim reapers with death shaped blade,
sulphuric breath chanting soon release.
They've bid their time,
devised their schemes,
practised precision on Hades' scores,
flaying and scraping,
cutting and carving,
gruesome figures with open sores.
Six fingered fiends,
extra strength to whip,
muscles and sinew cast taut,
imprisoned walled echoes of stamping feet,
they'll administer judgement as the nations weep.

These underworld principalities of sinister,
stewed slowly, deliberately to the boil,
to mix with all works of powers visible,
the whole globe to debauch, to despoil.
So this was the world,
a place of no truth or reality,
where even idolised rebels were found to be pawns.

Forget not the status of citizenry,
the billions removed from leaders games,
and Hail Fellow Merry,
he unnamed,
sculpting his sarcophagus in his own domain.

What we have thus far read you say,
this is the vastness of the world,
the unobtainable
where for most the dreams of ambition reside;
the macro,
where people knowingly exchange contentment's satisfaction
for a brief touch of glittering prize!

Herein, replied, hides sins contagion
where the innumerable stretch to covets reach,
collective integrity and charity released
for by their own hearts they self impeach.
They strive for gain,
for wants, not needs
becoming slow to share,
never attaining restful sleep,
sinking further toward abandons despair.

A fair observe you add in reply,
appears many consciences seared,
for self proves always right;
egos given fully to pride,
arrogance becoming their full delight.
Lamps bristling,
overflowing with abundant oils,
selling their mothers for a share of spoils.
Contemplate they not the destitute,
in affluent raiment walk by,
spurning desolations reach for a coin,
Samaritan spirit long void.
Generosity has left dilettante's town
to the cries of the poor they all turned blind.

Sin reigns; identifiable in the macro.
Sins scourge evident in all visible and unseen.

Sins damage destructs each nation, each townland.
Sins blemish distorts by home and by street.
Surely there is one found righteous?
Surely one finds a release escape?
Surely one remains chaste, found clean?
Surely one will not taste death?

Surely sin in one did tarry?
Perhaps observed in the tale of Hail Fellow Merry.

Hail Fellow Merry awoke alone upon the morn,
arranged he himself fair quick
after the cacophony of bells alarm,
one simple rule always at the ready:
see what for himself his day could reach.
Rushing at pace for door exit,
caught a glimpse,
in mirror caught his shape,
turned with haste to divert his eyes this trouble,
lest while looking he'd stumble upon his shame.

Cascaded forth his hearts imaginations,
motivations of inward leaving their stain,
weighed,
his own heart then found wanting,
attempted with detachment to buttress his disguise.
Memories attacked over deeds that required explaining,
an ambush sortie exposed ill treatment of friend,
his careers work agenda cutting corners for advantage,
self promoting manipulations bent to his will,
plans of others stolen secretly to fuel his ambition,
shouts of boast he'd heard himself proclaim.
Anger's cousin wrath against others he had kindled,
satisfying lusts; many indiscretions, many forgotten names.

Hail Fellow Merry had heard the lament of preachers,
he had listened callously, his heart remaining cold,
yet his conscience had been rent asunder
by the news of grace's triumph and eternal call.
Moved for just a hair breath second,
the unfortunate believed he had too much to lose,
he left the pulpit of eternals reckon,
too soon he said his wayward sins to cull.

Hail Fellow Merry is no different to all others,
he stopped, regrouped,
his reflection stared he down,
banished the opportunity to turn from his shame,
forced a crude fake smile and continued jauntingly upon his game.

The heart is wicked,
prone to deceive,
Shylock's pound corpuscle thin.
So what will happen I hear you say?
Fear not; God will weigh.

At some stage undetermined, unregistered,
before or after, no one knows,
Christ Jesus' believers disappeared.

The world rejoiced,
but not many even cared.

Part 2

Down the deep drowning

"Now I saw when the Lamb opened one of the seals,
and I heard one of the four living creatures
saying with a voice like thunder,
Come and see."

(Rev. 6:1.)

DOWN THE DEEP DROWNING

Down the deep drowning
wayward spirit of Cain,
broken fingered crawling
clawing to remain,
brooding on surface
fury from High,
casting His judgement;
all flesh to die.

Anger deep seething
grieving His heart,
yearned He for blessing
for grace to impart,
unrighteous endeavours
hastened smites pound,
waters prevailing,
rain's deepening abound.

The misery of sin
filled full its purse,
poisoning creation
with hates kill rage lust,
bloodied soil weeping
pleading end to man's curse,
down the deep drowning,
death to all lost.

This marked the first destruction;
restored later for fire.

Upon the trumpet on Mount Sinai tor,
displayed Yahweh His splendours power,
louder and louder the echo crescendoed,
until the Lord Himself descended.
Smoke and quake midst cloud and fire,
flash of lightening bright,
fearful, lest they perish, all Israel bowed,
The Almighty spoke from His unblemished light.

Hasten forward to end of ages
Heaven's glory will not be contained,
revealed by Christ in end-time pages,
the earth's demise long revealed.
The throne room of heaven casts no shadow
for by Blood all darkness subdued; erased.
Lightning strikes, shakes and thundering,
wide sea of full voiced praise,
seven lamps burning, the Spirits of God,
salvation's destination on open display.
Twenty four elders,
all clothed in white,
casting their crowns of gold,
four living creatures,
all surveying,
lion, calf, eagle, man; toward God all composed.
Omniscient, pre-existent,
The Creator, giver of life,
redeemed He His children, by love beckoned home,
shepherded safely by grace through faith.

Vengeances times' arrival promised from yore,
the Word's letters prophesied this age;
first tribulation,
wraths soon release,
the earth's epitaph by opened seal to engage.

Holy Trinity,
Deuteronomy's God in oneness union;
The God of Abraham, Isaac and Jacob,
ABBA Father turned to His Son.

"Why do the people plot and rage,
devise to hurry their ruin?
Through lack of knowledge they've all broken down
and judgement is soon coming.

Why do the nations scheme and weave,
hardened hearts become unyielding?
Vain conquests their foremost thought
yet Our justice comes quick wielding.

Why do the citizens of the globe turn cold
with hearts still warm beating?
All conscience it appears has run aground,
as Our revealed time approaches; soon nearing.

Our planets they march in measured path,
Our promise, abundant's glean,
seasons provide crops fruitful bounty
yet covets lust remains obscene.

Why do the peoples spurn our love?
Creators own blood pleading,
He given to death so all could live,
yet they err to idolatry's leaning.

Why through the construct of marshalled time,
where Our truth remains prevailing,
the next generation each age does spoil
with their ungodliness and false teaching?

Why do they take all that is good,
Sovereign's majesty and heart's desiring
and turn their backs to Throne's royal nod
to wallow in Eden's creeping?"

The Son contemplated His Father's yearning,
considered His opinion, His response then devised:
"Father Dearest, We gave Our Spirit,
but there is no fear of Us afore their eyes,
I walked the earth,
to You I pointed,
spoke at length upon repentances prize;
I shed My Blood on Calvary's cross,
three days later resurrected alive.
I took their guilt,
I paid their shame,
The Holy Spirit He came to dwell,
it appears however that they've chosen darkness
over new life created in My Holy Name.

All truth is seems they have abandoned,
they've floundered deep in tempest's tide,
served themselves in lavish squander,
bathed deep in flood swept pride.
As We survey each hidden secret,
My question Father.......
Is it time?"

"Who is able?"
roared an angel,
"this scroll to open, with seven seals.
Who is worthy?
Who is righteous?
Is there anyone here to fulfil our plead?"
Heaven's host cried,

their eyes diverted,
all around wondered who,
but then an elder, stepped he forward,
to The Lion of Judah he attention drew,
"Prevaileth He,
the Root of David.
Prevaileth He,
Heaven's Lamb that was slain.
Prevaileth He,
our gracious Saviour.
Prevaileth He
by His Blood by nail."

Ten thousand, ten thousand shook the heavens,
ten thousands more exclaimed worship praise,
thousands and thousands extolling His virtue,
each voice and heart to Him they raised.
The Son, He stood at His Father's beckon,
His right hand accepting eternity's scroll,
seven seals now to be broken,
seven seals heralding the turning from old.

Eternity's journey to earth but a twinkling
but from earth to heaven mostly four score years,
Heaven's eyes cast to earth's spinning shadow,
to a globe soon to be destroyed.
"Peace and safety," had become the nation's citation,
we are our own gods all hearts implied,
we need no Christ for our salvation
for Calvary's atonement they all despised.

Rust had corrupted, confined all under curse,
one inch below ground lived tribulations survey,
economics, technology, wars without ending,
disease and hunger announced impending fate.

For all the world toward greed had departed,
each restless soul sought a narcissists perch,
political leaders with voices all hollow
unknowingly committed their charges to dirt.

The Lord took the scroll to unseal the contents,
while earth drew breath on its last peaceful day.
Time became the smallest of minutes;
measured in horrors to claim justice's repay.

Four riders of wrath were prepared for the valley,
four riders of wrath,
death at the ready,
four riders of wrath commissioned for a journey
to birth the earth her doom.

Four riders of wrath the sound of horse echo,
armed with scythes and cold steel blades,
war and famine,
pestilence stalking,
four riders of wrath soon released for the end.

Four riders of wrath judgement not yielding,
to trample and churn the ground underfoot,
many miles to gallop,
these merciless warriors,
Heaven's judgement to chew up the dirt.

Four riders of wrath victims to pierce,
four riders of wrath to leave death in their wake,
behold a pale horse
for your name he is calling,
four riders of wrath will leave the whole globe dismayed.

Breaking the seals,
to unleash the riders,
trumpets and bowls soon into the fray,
four riders of wrath directed by watchers,
they'll despatch all heathen to hell bound graves.

Heaven succumbed to solemn silence,
The High Priest of confession stately stood,
alas anger kindled to white hot flame,
an audible crack from parchment heard,
The Word, The King, the first seal He opened,
a white house, its rider crowned with bow,
power to conquer his manifest order;
a sinful world to overthrow.

The decrepit world was thrice given over,
cauldrons chaos bubbling to boil,
society, institutions, the rule of government,
all that adjudicated now null and void.
Looting, rioting, mixed with murder,
split by ideologies, each one right,
factions falling from their self reliance,
all conspirators seeking power and might.
Fingers on red buttons, locked and loaded,
a nuclear holocaust perhaps to unveil,
descent to darkness and utter madness,
a question arose - who can save?

Strongmen arose midst peers and equals,
insurrection words and plotted betrayals,
none could master all knowing wisdom,
all who tried over a short time failed.
The whole world came under the sway of wicked,
surely someone sane would prevail,
in all the clandestine no good did triumph,
none called on He who bled by nail.

Hail Fellow Merry observed the confusion,
joined in the chorus of those who wailed,
wished a return to his normal existence,
for from nowhere his movements had become curtailed.
Locked under law, the same every nation,
strictest of measures propagated in authority's name,
his years suspended to forlorn and frenzy,
he yearned for passion; he missed his games.
While under the cosh, the threat of war,
a solution enforcer; a man of peace.
Come world give your allegiance,
for your freedom choose antichrist.

Arose a man of Assyrian root,
exalting himself above every god,
Abraham, Isaac and Seed despised,
a vile speaker of blasphemy words.
Held he no regard for the God of Israel,
no fondness either for women bright,
self composed, demanding worship,
seized he his kingdom by works of slight.
Crafty this wordsmith and wily of fox,
his knowledge exceeded all sages of old,
the earth flocked anxiously to serve her new master,
this prince of darkness of underworld.

By peace with words his war he waged,
acknowledged he foreign gods and their public display,
his now the sanctuary at last to defile,
desolation of abomination; Antiochus Epiphanes replayed.
Confirmed he a covenant, a week of years,
watch out! At the midpoint his terms he will change;
empowered by satan for a time of ending,
for by this worm God's wrath be played.
Given charge a time by Almighty,

he'll cut off the sheltered, the anointed by blade will depart,
he'll supervise the laurels of all temporal power
and perish all fruit by his arrogant heart.

At some stage Christ Jesus' believers disappeared.
All entire world rejoiced but not many even cared.

Earth dwellers observe the physical realm
but behind the veil another dimension,
the Spirit world, a place of God's dominion
additionally a war perpetrated by angels long fallen.
The earth replicates this spiritual domain,
times of peace coupled with wars of distortion,
while Yahweh's clock is purposed toward His sovereign,
remember the opening of seals begins God's hour of judgement.

"Come and see," announced the second living creature,
Christ Jesus has opened the scroll's second seal,
another horse accompanied by rider,
great sword wielding from fiery red steed.
Neighing steam nostrils, rage horse sweat bathed,
unleashing the reins the rider death dressed,
directing movement toward desolation,
war on earth, an end to earth's peace.

Cymbals crashing, heavy as thunder,
kingdom against kingdom from prophecy page,
carnage, attrition, death and dishonour,
the innocent not spared the rider's sword rage.
Israel the target her enemies roaring,
strong armies from north, from east and from west,
Goliath against David, the mission destruction,
The Lord has however His own stones to cast.

Gog of Magog, Meshech and Tubal,
Persia, Ethiopia, Libya armed to the teeth,
Gomer, Togarmah, troops by the legion
hooks in their mouths, The Lord will their end complete.
Worldwide the nations drawn to battle,
the globe plunged into darkness, His misery to unfold,
hells release of dread the red buttoned missiles,
Zechariah remembered as flesh dissolved blue.
Cities and town lands, streets pulled asunder,
bomb blast biting, cutting to bone,
death cries and mayhem, blood drench wound anger,
the birthing of chaos, the delivery of doom.
Communities stricken by brass hail of bullet,
no discretion in aiming all in sights fell,
unless one called on sinning man's Saviour
perishing souls all departed for hell.

Through the streets ran Hail Fellow Merry,
his district spared the shockwave screams,
through broken glass and rough sharp rubble
he darted low out of snipers reach.
"Wars are for history," he thought as he lumbered,
"what happened my life? Why am I here?"
no answer he found in his deep brain rumblings,
trying to stay alive became his chief care.

He searched the streets, he passed dead corpses,
looking for someone, anyone he knew,
he spotted a few long known acquaintances
pulverised dead; a bomb had they slew.
He sought out dry shelter and some sticks for warming,
he slept in a drainpipe fending off vermin's sting bite,
he woke at night screaming, his tears ran in silence,
"how long more?" he wondered "and most of all why?"

Lying in wait antichrist pondered,
his move he would make but at the right time,
peace and assurance through political manoeuvring
positioning himself for meteoric rise.
The citizenry all hailed him, a man of works wondrous,
the media broadcast him for of calm spoke his voice,
the unholy alliance endorsed him their riches now rusting,
for at last for a dying world a face all could trust.

At some stage Christ Jesus' believers disappeared.
The entire world rejoiced but not many even cared.

Daily they arrived in the stronghold of Heaven,
under His Wings the saved took flight,
Heavens sanctuary, safe secure refuge,
sinners forgiven, their bounty His delight.
Upon a promontory Christ Jesus stood forward,
observed He the machinations of His earthly domain,
knew He from infinity those who would call,
full atonement offered freely through grace in His Name.

With scroll still in hand the third seal He cracked open,
on earth they hoped end but this still the commence,
a third horse, black, deep colour of midnight,
the rider with scales, weight balanced in hands.
Black was the colour; obsidian chalice.
Black was the colour; famine to reign.
Black was the colour; rooting out sins hiding.
Black was the colour; all to taste death.

Summer scorch burning then winters deep drowning
destroying the farmlands as harvests grew thin,
freezing ice winds and land racked by bomb blast,
wheatland sodden and ploughed by wars grim.
Vegetation destroyed, the animals started dying,

no grass for feed on earth's scalded crust,
judgement scales, a day's wage for eating
if one could find crops through scraping the dirt.

Antichrist remained safe midst his stores of plenty,
his minions, they he serving; they hoping he'd save,
cracked he his whip as the masses toiled in labour,
like Pharaoh of old much wealth he did glean.
He demanded output and pounded dissention,
measured their food by quart for their wage,
spurned all counsel favouring cruel punishment,
then sat back satisfied as the fat grew lean.

Malnutrition bites slow as ones rib cage grows tighter,
stomachs distending as eyes bulge through skull,
limbs waste then, strength ebbs out faster,
weakened steps linger as pace nears its dust.
Tiredness prevails as hope can go no further,
not much reserve left midst death and disease,
then memory assaults as one tastes past feeding,
sudden descent to grave is famines last wheeze.

Hail Fellow Merry killed his first human,
a child sadly carrying a small slice of bread,
hit he this innocent with a rock piece deep bruising,
scoffing his spoil as the boy drew last breath.
No conscience days mourning for Hail Fellow Merry,
continued his way, streets littered with dead,
inside the ruins loud voices moaning,
crying, pleading an end to the dread.

Each is capable of acts horrendous,
all culpable at Majesty's charge,
for from the deepest of emotions reservoir
self serve ignites the detonating charge.

As regards sin a recidivist,
Hail Fellow Merry more blood he did sate,
though he never attacked one his own size standing,
he murdered plenty to fill his plate.

Thus far a leader,
his wars did he wage,
then famine and hunger,
economic collapse.
The world kept fast spinning,
under Thunder's decree,
nowhere to hide,
nowhere to flee.

At some stage Christ Jesus' believers disappeared.
The entire world was weary; they no even longer cared.
"Come and see," proclaimed the fourth living creature,
in The Lord's presence he bowed low in love,
vengeance on sin still at The Lords beckon,
His plan long revealed now ushered more blood.
Justice was paramount, revenge the quest,
one either died slow or one died fast,
behold a pale horse, seal number four,
on its back black Death and Hades dark rode.

Hunger expunged, obliterated the many,
murder on rampage midst cities of rot,
harbingers of hell roast, constant pain numbing,
scavengers hunting, scouting for crumbs.
Economic hardship, no value in money,
high denomination currency just good to burn,
nothing to buy, shelves depleted and empty,
assets valueless as creditors left spurned.

No escape whatever one's standing,
no class distinction as death ploughed its ground,
men in gold towers, glass topped Babels,
found no protection; often self end sealing their tombs.
No matter the country, no matter the city,
the horseman stalked streets with rapier blade,
no segregation in race, no chasm dividing,
apart from the antichrist all earths systems failed.

A fourth of earth fell by end the fourth judgement,
two billion died and many more ill,
four riders of wrath all regions now patrolling,
administering justice, quickening the damned.
Rotting, not buried, decomposing carcases,
piled on street corners, bruised ulcerated black,
pyres burning, flame and smoke ascending,
prevailing stink sending juice stench to sky.

At some stage Christ Jesus' believers disappeared.
Hail Fellow Merry cursed God; he would not Christ Jesus serve.

The alliance of wicked colluded for ruin,
death to the followers, the servants of God,
eradicate The Lord and His Holy presence,
we desire this world for our very own laud.
Antichrist and false prophet agreed barbarous slaughter,
hatching and plotting iniquitous scheme,
execute them eviscerate them, hide them, just kill them,
get rid of The Word's scourge by any foul means.

To prisons constructed they rounded the righteous,
carnal jailhouses became the stomp ground of death,
loyalists to this new world regime sought out work,
many took jobs to excoriate breath.

Hail Fellow Merry became one such functionary,
took a role for three squares a day,
spared he no quarter killing the innocent,
found he gloried in bloodlust; a new game to play.

This fifth seal opened spelt death for the righteous,
for followers of Christ whose Word they held dear,
execution without trial became their rite of passage,
afore leaving this world many testimonies shared.
The prison camps a production line horror,
those targeted just quietly disappeared,
under cover darkness troops came and raided,
those left, the unrighteous, stood back and cheered.

Joint heirs with Christ had warned and admonished,
like Noah of old they had spoken to warn,
they had witnessed The Messiah and His judgement impending,
all flesh had been warned afore The Lord's ire.
Slain for believing, their crime free salvation,
executed without reason millions shed blood,
minded they not deaths final incarceration,
for by grace they promised new creation's home above.
Welcomed to Heaven, clothed in white robes,
joined by those who antichrist's actions slew,
Old Testament heroes singing God's praises,
New Testament warriors birthed anew.
The multitudes of Heaven turned to their Saviour,
gathered together their voices they raised,
"How long our Sovereign? Holy and True Name,
avenge Thou our blood; Your wrath please display."

The Lord loved His own, He cherished His children,
His Spirit kindled on each tongue of flame,
beckoned them rest in midst His Holy,
announced He to all "A few more to save."

"Come rest while longer," he quietly encouraged,
"My final number is not yet home,
antichrist will kill as many as We've given,
your fellow servants will worship soon at My Throne."

At some stage the end of the time of gentiles was ushered.
Hail Fellow Merry hardened his heart further against God.

The finest of parchment, scroll's sacred rolled leather,
thick leaf of substance lined straight and true,
crafted by hand afore earth's creation,
calligraphy printed with inks rich in blue.
The seals honey waxed clothed by wax candle,
embossed with the signet of Heaven's Royal King,
The Lord took the scroll and broke the sixth seal,
they fearful on earth the dread it would bring.

No time of rest for earth's battle weary,
no time to regroup, no restoration worldwide,
no time to wallow in sadness or mourning,
each day that dawned brought more blight to survive.
"What will come next?" the beaten wondered,
even antichrist knowing his fate the result he denied,
"Is it my time to die?" queried each person,
ragged and torn, staring wide-eyed.

It started slow but then to quick rumble,
the ground it quaked from deep underneath,
the caverns of darkness and chasms of lava,
sprung they all forth from dormant of sleep.
From all around the earth's crust exploded,
rattling and moaning each hemisphere recoiled,
shooting forth rocks and fragments of poison,
death was flung high out of sky's reach.

Dirt and dust, noxious flame plumes
blocked all vision, the sun bleak black grew,
all standing, all nature descended to chaos,
then blood was the colour, the hue of the moon.
The winds blew in fury exercised He His might,
all the globe shaking and breaking like glass,
elements distorted melting in deep groaning,
sin scalded burning at sound of seal's blast.

Day drew to closing, no night song this evening,
the stars of heaven fell from the sky,
Zodiac's partners, eighty eight constellations,
dissolved in a frisson of celestial fire.
The sky receded like a tide of great waters,
tsunami of shaking and quaking and boil,
every mountain and island was moved without warning,
many were killed in uprooting turmoil.

The kings of the age thought they'd rule forever,
the rich men, the great men, commanders of earth,
joined they this time by the bonded and freemen,
trying to find shelter in caves under rocks.
They knew it was Jesus, Royal King of Heaven,
they knew it was judgement for their very sins,
they begged for death each one in hiding,
urging the boulders to fall and them kill.
Hail Fellow Merry included in number,
ran he through carnage fast on his feet,
ducking and diving clawing through ditches,
no end in sight his trial not yet complete.
He heard the ground rumbling, opening behind him,
to a dank cave he made it, nare turned around,
clasping his chest he fought long for lung breath,
all strength exhausted in cavern's surround.

Great and awesome this day of The Lord,
Joel's prophecy of old teaching realised,
a great day of wrath those under curse judgement,
a great day of joy for those few saved.
Heaven's throne room stood silent in reverence,
voices hushed for just a short time,
terrible this earthly scene, peregrination from Almighty,
who is able, able to stand?

At some stage the ruination of the sixth seal ended.
Those left alive hardened their hearts toward The Living God.

In the beginning God created the heavens and the earth,
let Us make man in Our image declared the sixth day,
then fall did man, tempered with full knowledge sin,
calamity's destruction leaving a world broken at its very begin.
Never the less God by grace did intervene,
blessed Abraham, a nation he decreed,
blessed eternal, Abraham promised soon a son,
judged righteous for by faith Abraham Yahweh believed.

Jacob to his son Joseph was late restored,
upon foreign soil in Egypt his sons he gathered round,
twelve boys now men, the host of Israel's tribe,
for each a word afore Isaac's sons time grew thin.
Words of prophecy, of blessing and of warn,
for each son and for a time future too revealed,
Jacob soon departed, his forefathers he joined,
buried in family plot, before Mamre in Machpelah's field.

Pharaoh was hardened, swept away in Red Sea tide,
Moses led all Israel but upon Mount Nebo died,
crossing the Jordan, on anointed ground Joshua stood,
not a word failed; Yahweh was wholly faithful to His truth.
An everlasting covenant promised the Lord's anoint,

twelve tribes through generations blessed by God's own Word,
seventieth week of Daniel, Israel's remnant The Lord will save,
confirmed by Paul in Romans; Yahweh's covenant will prevail.

Silence cast a shadow on earth's thorn cursed ground,
those alive, who survived, stopped awhile and paused.
"Perhaps this an end! Perhaps we can rebuild!
Build back better possibly!" wondering if from fear they now released.
But God stood back perused His work, His Word He must fulfil,
sent He four angels out, the winds of earth to still,
another angel, The Seal of God purposed for this hour,
144,000 of Israel's foreheads to seal by Salvation's gracious power.

Twelve thousand of the tribe of Judah the angel he did seal.
Twelve thousand of the tribe of Reuben.
Twelve thousand of the tribe of Gad.
Twelve thousand of the tribe of Asher.
Twelve thousand of the tribe of Naphtali.
Twelve thousand of the tribe of Manasseh.
Twelve thousand of the tribe of Simeon.
Twelve thousand of the tribe of Levi.
Twelve thousand of the tribe of Issachar.
Twelve thousand of the tribe of Zebulun.
Of Joseph, the stolen son, twelve thousand foreheads sealed.
Of Benjamin, a favoured son, twelve thousand foreheads sealed.

Salvation belongs to our God Heaven's multitude sang,
all nations, peoples and tongues clothed in robe bright white,
all angels, living creatures and elders stood,
bowing before The Lord's throne to worship.
Robes washed white in the Blood of The Lamb,
great tribulation took their earthly lives,
while on earth for most of remain,
their hearts did The Lord despise.

Opened to silence the seventh Seal while the Lord's anointed stood,
seven angels of God's royal guard handed seven trumpets,
another angel with the prayers of the saints in hand a golden censer
from the altar he took fire and cast it to earth in judgement.
Wrath released in midst of quake,
violent shaking heralding slaughter,
still Hail Fellow Merry could not repent,
his heart calloused black by his Maker.

Part 3

Down the deep spiral

"So the seven angels who had the seven trumpets prepared themselves to sound."

(Rev. 8:6.)

DOWN THE DEEP SPIRAL

down
down
down

Down the deep spiral,
craftily engineered from your youth.

down
down
DOWN

Down the deep spiral,
ingeniously designing you to fit a mould.

down
DOWN
DOWN

Down the deep spiral,
each to play their role.

DOWN
DOWN
DOWN

Down the deep spiral,
wrath will take its toll.

Down, down, down the deep spiral,
death's harvester is at the door.
Fear God!
He has done it all before.

The noise;
deafening.
A calamitous roar.

The outermost;
rumbling, quaking,
shaking from the deep of earth's bubbling core.

The ground;
splitting,
heaving,
vomiting debris forth.

Those surviving,
in caves hiding,
each afraid,
scared to move.

Hail Fellow Merry sat in dark,
alone,
unobserved in pitch,
tartarian blanket dreadful black,
consumed his frame that night.
This stygian crypt dull in gloom,
cavern of ruin unlit,
dank, musty, cruel cruel air,
through gasps he'd breathe in grit.
Gnashing of teeth,
no candlelight,
face covered in blood and spit.
This pusillanimous man,
terrified bleak,
mute of voice,
afraid to speak.

Could be morning
or hour of night,
no light shadow cast from sun or moon,
wails and groans and midnight screams,
slaughter's birth of death starved doom.
Surrounding cries from flesh unseen,
shattered egos, broken bones,
terrified to move,
no aid to seek,
pitiful, pathetic,
alone.
No bond these people
except for death,
no sanctuary from long lost home.

In white shock rot,
he clung to rocks,
his mind unhinged,
unsealed,
he drew deep breaths,
then rubbed his frame,
numbed bones
quick warmed to feel.
He dared to stand,
this broken ground,
flat shelf he found to lie
and closed his eyes
and wished to die,
last sleep to draw full nigh.

In dreamlike trance
he found some rest
to childhood his mind replayed,
saw his parents,
vague silhouettes,

their love he tried embrace,
here his house,
his school, some friends,
his life coursed through his years.
Then suddenly afore,
on hallowed ground,
a steeple caught his eye,
a warming voice,
doorways entice,
encouraged him inside
and sitting down
on pew wood brown
Preachers plead came prompting ear.

Eloquence of preaching,
words in fluid motion building,
oratory sublime,
collected thoughts,
joining dots,
reasoned well with rhyme.

"Therefore, in conclusion," encouraged the Preacher,
"our text again, John 3:18,
he who believes in Him is not condemned,
but
he who does not believe is condemned already
because he has not believed in the Name
of the only begotten Son of God.

Jesus Christ; the express image of The Father.
Jesus Christ; the incarnate glory of Heaven sent.
Jesus Christ; the mercy of sinners fallen.
Jesus Christ; Forgiver of sins saves you by His grace through faith.

Jesus Christ; the Creator eternal.
Jesus Christ resurrected frees you from the punishment of death.
Jesus Christ; a Saviour to the unworthy,
Jesus Christ; the Judge of all living, the Judge of all dead.

Jesus Christ; it is He whom we worship.
Jesus Christ; it is He our prayers beseech.
Prophet of prophets, Royal King, High Priest eternal,
Jesus Christ to His glory we freely reach.

Your choice to repent will shepherd you safely to Heaven,
there thou shalt reside to worship at His Throne,
your other choice, nothing quotidian,
alas my friends......hell's abject oblivion."

Hail Fellow Merry tingled,
his reaction brought surprise,
heartened by his hearing
he rushed to claim his prize.
Two words caught attention,
two words warmed his frame within,
the first word - abject,
the second - oblivion.

He held no regard this Jesus.
To serve another - No!
To repent - What of!
To turn from sin - Hell no!
Oblivion sounded exciting,
to this race he would place his bet
then run this course with fury pace,
wagering all against God's threats.

That evening now remembered,
a sultry, humid night,
the Preachers' yearnings recollected
from a state of stark regret,
to turn the clock years backward
from oblivions dissolute breath
for satan that night did stake his claim
and will soon collect his debt.

It is quicker to die in the open
than hide in cavern dark
so outside Hail Fellow Merry ventured
hoping this his final hour.
He found an eyrie cliff top
to engage this feast of eyes
to witness Eternal's reckon
as trumpets filled the skies.

Suddenly without warning
Heaven's glory filled the air,
Hark! A trumpet noise
echoed everywhere.
Like a sound of noon day gun blast
Heaven's sound shook living bones,
an angel mixed hail, fire and blood
then flung wrath to earth's scorched ground.
Designed to destroy vegetation
the earth's great grasslands were targeted by ire,
from South Americas grand Pampas,
to Northern Prairies
and fields afar.
Mongolia and Tibet to Manchuria's heave of green,
all green grass was burnt,
all vegetation
and one third of earth's born trees.

No food then for roaming wildness,
Africa's big five starved quick on feet,
great swathes of the animal kingdom
wiped away with fury zeal.
No more ground for farming cereal,
no more hope for finding food,
depletion of earth's oxygen
as carbon slowly brewed.
Historically fire had devastated regions
but never on such scale
and yet those who remained refused to call
on Him that bled by nail.

This was no Hollywood scripted movie,
sequenced events transpired in time,
as quick the first trumpet ended
the second sounded rhyme.
Another angel sounded
and a great mountain burning with fire
was thrown to the sea,
devastating repercussions near and far.

There is no Neptune for protection,
no Poseidon of the seas,
Pontus is of the imagination;
no false water deities.
Judgement is from Yahweh
and Christ Jesus His only begotten Son,
no vain hope found in anything elsewhere
no false gods of deep ocean
and when His wrath hit water
one third the seas turned to blood,
one third of all sea creatures were killed,
one third of ships undone.

All dead sank to the depths of darkness,
shielded far from vague slim light,
the second trumpet blowing,
crashing waters unloosing blight.

More accurate trumpet third,
more precise than light the speed of rock,
times infinity the volume,
one hundred fold the shock.
Tremors and thunders,
blood shot roar,
this star slung from tumult's store.
Pebbles and dash,
fierce, fierce heat,
to pummel and crash,
dislodge earth's feet,
foundations ripped to deep root core,
never ever seen before.
With crashing cymbals from archer's strings,
fiery arrows and snake bite stings,
rattles and moans,
gravity's broken bonds
for from disobedience's curse one cannot abscond.
Fury from High this speed of ball
seen on ground by those left to fall,
they shook their fists,
they called Him names,
hastened then quick to hell bound graves.
Misery's world beat by stick,
the whole cursed earth,
the whole head sick.

Wormwood,
created,
birthed star of stone,
constructed fore earths first living breath was formed,
trajectory's pathway,
trundled along,
timed to perfection for trumpets song.
Wormwood's collision,
destruction on the roam,
one third of freshwater springs and rivers,
this burning ember star,
waters corrupted in Wormwood soak,
many dying from poison's choke.

All that was created
was then by God curtailed,
the fourth angel trumpet sounded,
another judgement was revealed.
One third the sun was darkened,
one third the moon destroyed,
one third of stars were stained,
one third of day did not shine.
Below a globe in chaos,
each hemisphere recoiled,
for the whole world a time of blackness,
one third the heavenly realm spoiled.
An angel flew midst Heaven,
resonant in voice,
woe, woe, woe to earth's inhabitants,
from remaining trumpet blasts.

Hail Fellow Merry was rendered speechless,
against sharp cleft rock he edged his back,
in all his comprehension
he could not envisage the next attack.

Smoke rose thick and choking
all vision bruised from sight,
shepherding hidden locust demons
from darkness out to light.
Smoke ascended from the depths,
Abaddon's soldiers armed,
poison in their tails
as fifth trumpets woe found start.
Smoke swirled grey and yellow
from the darkest cavern trail,
locusts to the battle
to sting with pointed tail.

The bottomless pit was opened
from heat's furnace underground
releasing judgements locusts
for their sting bite to abound.
For those unsealed from Heaven
a bite on body frame,
five months of burning torment,
no death reprieve of grave.

Five months to hurt men fallen.
Five months of stinged payback.
Five months of deep flesh cutting.
Five months of excruciating attack.

Hidden in eyrie cliff top
Hail Fellow Merry felt he safe
but pointed out by Apollyon
a locust bit his face.
He screamed and roared in turmoil,
he cursed Yahweh from his heart
and wrestled in his torture,
for five months he fell apart.

The first woe found its ending,
its completion the unsealed did plead,
however from justices reckon
the sixth trumpet was released.

Almighty, Almighty Holy God,
Yahweh from His domain approved His royal decree,
holy angels, authority in hand
at an exact hour afore ordained.
More precise than Wormwood,
four angels river bound,
Euphrates keepers discharged,
death to kill a world's third.

Two hundred million the army of woe.
Two hundred million the whole world to plough.

Fire, smoke and brimstone,
mouths like lions,
across the hemispheres,
scything, rapier quick dying.
This second woe catapulting dread,
this sixth trumpet,
the release of death.

One third the earth died by gruesome,
injury, disease multiplied,
since opening of judgement a hefty price paid,
close to five billion people by wrath swept away.

Sin's reward gleaned full her purse,
for sins leaning enjoys a rapacious thirst,
then closed at its end the sixth trumpet full spent,
those remaining alive still refused to repent.

Meanwhile antichrist,
his plan he did reveal,
kill The Lord's anointed
by cunning and deceit.
He drew the imagination of all peoples
in allegiance fidelity they swore,
this man of war,
disguised by peace
at this the earths last hour.
With hierarchical pyramid
he administered and surveilled,
seven heads,
ten regions
he in a position unassailed.

Unfettered delusion
his currency of power,
the nations at his whim
as tribes and peoples bowed,
him they chose,
this despoiler of unbridled grim.
He ruled his kingdom,
much chaos he did muster,
murdered,
plundered,
ravaged all,
arrayed in dark;
death's shadow.

Clever and deceptive
to him all terrified bowed,
afraid they'd die,
if he they denied,
all liberty cast askew.
He ruled by fear

but it of iron clay,
brittle to the touch
all soon prone to decay,
destined to drown in flame.
But until that hour of reckon,
craftily he wore his mask,
destroying,
hastening death
with his tight mercurial grip.

No voice of reasoned dissension,
no sense of debate engaged,
even the kings of the earth drew back
in case their own fate he sealed.

To The Lord's city
which the pretender had defiled,
Yahweh, Eternal Father
two witnesses He empowered.
Three and half years they witnessed prophecy
and like Moses in pharaoh's court
they dealt with evil principalities
while demonstrating Yahweh's hope.
But when their testimony ended
behold from the bottomless pit,
power given to the beast
the two witnesses to kill.
Citizens rose to rejoicing,
their nemesis in defeat,
yet God allowed continued mockery
then resurrected the two witnesses to their feet.

Ascended the witnesses to Heaven,
fear fell upon Jerusalem's ground,
an earthquake hit the city
a tenth the citadel fell down.

The second woe was over,
numb now those left on streets,
behold Eternal Majesty,
the seventh trumpet then released.

Worship praise to Holy God
unveiled by seventh sound,
control that had been wilfully relinquished
returned whole to Yahweh's power.
Twenty four elders bowed at Throne,
Holy Trinity they magnified
and casting all restraint by The Spirit rejoiced
with thanksgiving of worship joy.
Sustained He by grace His glorious saints
and for judgement the purveyors of death,
two peoples evidenced through history's course;
those who fear Jacob's God and those who perpetrated dread.

Heaven's temple of God was opened,
His ark of covenant seen,
great lightening, thundering, great Heavenly signs,
Yahweh's power to earth released.

An ivory tower is the boast of kings,
issuing orders to bid their killings,
butchers and brigands they send out in quest,
ambitious cut-throats their kings they try impress.

Herod was one such psychopath,
deranged by glint of gold,
Magi gentiles told him of a new King born,
Herod's reaction in scripture foretold.
To Ramah Herod sent strength to kill
but not an invading army's blood to spill,

but lo! Young babes became his threat,
gold, frankincense, myrrh not gifted: but death.
Boys of age, all under two,
guilty mercenaries, these goliaths slew,
parading streets and poor folks homes,
they stabbed with spear and bloodied swords.
A brave man this Herod!
A worldly, mighty man,
unfortunately not one of a kind,
for history boasts these criminal kings
and in historys pages only killing you will find.

Woe to the inhabitants of the earth,
the beast,
the dragon is here,
possessing antichrist, Israel's sealed then fled for sanctuary,
so the devil enraged pursued other offspring,
those who God, they alone do fear.

Blood and testimony; they overcomers.
Blood and testimony; their lives laid down.
Blood and testimony; not long for this world.
Blood and testimony; the saints marched home.

In the years that preceded,
the unholy trinity tried to have their way,
half of them, in human form, demons,
the remaining erev rav became satan's prey.
Weak people with no souls,
their integrity, miry clay,
enjoyed they the trappings of engagement
but in the end all swept away.
None mentioned sinning man's Saviour,
those who did were voted out of power,
for the nations, the peoples hated Christ Jesus
and chose to wither like autumn's last flower.

Blasphemy's beast assumed total control,
the peoples marvelled at his temporal power,
forty two months he granted authority,
to execute the righteous with great zeal in his ire.
Those not named in the King's Book of Life
with great gusto followed this man,
swore their allegiance to this hell bound fiend
and took his mark at his demand.

Six. Six. Six; remarkable signs and wonders.
Six, Six. Six; with cunning deceit.
Six, Six. Six; the number of satan.
Six, Six. Six; right hand stamped receipt.

Rich man and poor took his engraving,
free and slave; forehead or hand?
No buying or selling for those not receiving,
they gifted and accepted blade's scaffold stand.

And what do you say of Hail Fellow Merry?
Did he find salvation before his demise?
How could one continue in deception?
Surely the trumpets opened his eyes!

His mind cast back once more to his childhood,
while sitting on his ledge he remembered the barn,
corrugated iron painted with gray top,
sitting aside his Grandfather's farm.
Framed in gun metal,
dark as the night mist,
entry doorway
dark encased.
The young boy felt it the doorway to demons,
with squealing noise echoes
as the door was pushed back,

metal on metal grating his memory,
engaged wheels screamed shaking his core;
the entrance like teeth chomping and biting
seeking a child, someone to devour.
Then through this chasm he walked on his lonesome,
coals piled high for homes furnace fire,
wood, straw and kindling stacked to the brim top
soon to smoulder like death's end day prowl.
If bold as a child he was sent to this cauldron,
wailing door sealed him like graves dug ditch tomb,
no matter how long he tried to erase this memory
his imagination continued to stoke all his fears.

So now the whole world became one big barn door,
misty black bleak extinguished all hope,
at first he defiant
then fear built a stronghold,
he followed all rhetoric
and selling his soul accepted satan's mark.

No turning back now for Hail Fellow Merry,
destination of hell now his guarantee,
never again a chance for repentance,
free grace salvation vanished like breeze.

First fruits to God,
144,000,
worship and praise,
sealed they by God.
Redeemed from men,
undefiled virgins,
a new song they sung,
in the throne room of God.

Another angel
flying midst Heaven,
everlasting gospel
preached with a loud voice.
Another angel
announcing Babylon has fallen,
a third angel warned those marked,
fire and brimstones reward for their vice.

Behold a white cloud,
one like the Son of Man,
seated,
golden crowned.
Commanded He His angels
to sickle and reap earths harvest;
one angel His children gathered,
another angel those for everlasting weep.

What started in Heaven
journeyed full circle,
there multitudes gathered
by The Lord's own anoint.
One of the four living creatures
gave seven bowls to seven angels;
the last judgements;
final plagues of indignation and wrath.

Part 4

Down the deep dying

"Then I saw another sign in heaven,
great and marvellous;
seven angels having the seven last plagues,
for in them the wrath of God is complete."

(Rev. 15:1.)

DOWN THE DEEP DYING

Raised high
in box wood ply,
pallbearers erect
square shouldered,
lowered down
walled dirt surround
despatched
eternal hereafter.

Down the deep dying
where humans don't belong.

Oh why, Oh why
must all men die?
death skulking
around each corner,
most to hell
at deaths toll bell
thereafter
devil's slaughter.

Down the deep dying
where humans don't belong.

Oh wake up men
ye sons of Cain
avoid
damnations wallow,
take charge yer bairns
encourage them The Lord to follow,
for folly will issue a cruel receipt
and unquenchable is hell's swallow.

Bang.
Bang.
Bang.
Seven coffin nails.

Bang.
Bang.
Bang.
Judgements full assail.

Bang.

Full pounded meat cleaver.

Seven broken seals,
seven trumpets then revealed.
Afore all is finished
the last seven will be unveiled.

Now such a predicament the world had never seen before,
all because The Creator, Saviour from their hearts they chose ignore.
Made they themselves their own gods
of metal and of stone
and bowed beneath these dead things
as ambitions turned to groans.

Sin is resilient,
I fear it is how we are shaped
as we yearn to cut corners
and forget to practice grace.
Such is the way of humans
we fall and fail again
but Christ Jesus rose victorious
for sinners He came to save.

To learn about the future
one must visit history past,
to investigate and comprehend,
to discern antichrist types.
Subsequent then judgement
for through sufferings we toil
then are drawn either to repentance
or to judgements last turmoil.

To understand Revelation
to Exodus you must go
and trace Yahweh's dealings
with the Hebrews of ago.

By faith through Abraham
the promise of nation bestowed,
not just land
but for His people a home.
A righteous man this Abraham
he learnt to follow The Lord,
walked and talked with his Saviour,
at one in communions accord.
The Lord informed Abraham of the future,
in famine to Egypt Israel would flee,
four hundred years later to return
when the Amorites wickedness was complete.
In time The Lord sent first Joseph,
a prisoner in chains,
later elected to Prime Minister
when he Pharaoh's dreams explained.
Sanctuary for his family
Joseph did later provide,
seventy of Jacob
found refuge during hungers plight.

Four centuries later another Pharaoh arose,
one whom Israel's history he did not know,
this Pharaoh plagued God's people,
worked them to the bone
stripping wealth and substance,
finally Yahweh heard their groans.
The Sovereign of all history
deemed it time to bring them home.

These Hebrews, chosen and freed by God,
favoured in Joseph by Pharaoh of old,
usurped by time becoming slaves,
put under dominion,
broken,
distressed and exposed.

Raised Yahweh Moses,
a Prince of royal Egyptian court,
saved by God Almighty,
Hebrew by birth.
In taking a stand for God's people,
Moses had to flee,
forty years in the wilderness,
prepared for destiny.

Go you to Pharaoh
God to Moses spoke
and speak under My command,
"Let My people go!"
It was Yahweh's desire
Pharaoh's heart to expose
then to release His children,
His people whom I AM chose.

To the royal court Moses travelled,
explained he God's desire
but Pharaoh thought himself a god
and hardened his resolve.
Pharaoh multiplied the labours
of the chosen Hebrew race
but Yahweh came with judgement,
released at vector's pace.

Pharaoh is a type of antichrist,
he had power to rule his day,
subjugated bowed before him
and his taxes they did pay.
Pharaoh's priests did signs and wonders
felt he in sovereign control
until Yahweh stretched His hand
to smite Egypt's king of old.

Like in Revelation
Yahweh undertook plagues release,
Egypt had ten solemn judgements
to eradicate Pharaoh's seat.
Each plague was a physical manifestation
with a spiritual dimension attached,
to crumble the foundation of temporal man;
idolatry's curse to be smashed.

False gods were the target
of Yahweh's sovereign might
but at no stage did Pharaoh
soften heart to the Hebrew's toil or plight.

The first plague turned waters to blood,
no drinking water or fish to eat for miles.
This was a judgement on Osiris,
pagan deity of the Nile.

The second plague saw frogs upon the ground,
a blanket of slimy filth and putrid stink distress.
This was a judgement upon Hekt,
Egypt's frog goddess.

The third plague, Lice,
with an itch of no depart.
This was a judgement upon Seb,
Egypt's god of earth.

Swarms of flies became plague number four,
yet God's people in Goshen did not suffer strife.
This was a judgement on Hatkok,
Osiris' goddess wife.

Economic and religious life was targeted,
the fifth plague where livestock became diseased.
Pharaoh's heart was hardened; he did not let them go,
this a determined judgement on Egypt's bull god Apis.

Next leprous pus-filled boils fell upon each man,
occurred when Moses scattered ash which fell upon the land.
Yahweh hardened the heart of Pharaoh
and judged Egypt's god Typhon.

Number seven - hail,
hitting herb and tree.
Shu, god of the atmosphere judged
while Goshen escaped all misery.

The eighth plague revealed locusts that chewed upon the land,
east winds scavenge devouring bounty crust.
This was a judgement on Serapia,
Egypt's protector from locusts.

Pharaoh's heart was by God further hardened
as the ninth plague stretched its hold.
Darkness, deep deep blackness
against Ra, the sun god, crawled upon the ground.

Finally the firstborn
died in every home.
During the first Passover God saved His people,
under blood in each their homes.

Weighed heavily,
Pharaoh's stone heart
drowned his bones,
killed stone cold dead
by Yahweh's extend of arm,
he allowed a short span,
his lusts to wage his war,
yet his last day was never within his power.

Evil folks,
committing their paths to self,
many antichrists,
over many centuries passed,
killing God's anointed,
by pogrom, gun and fire,
killing each their millions
to serve their own desires.

Such the way of men,
beginning to the end,
Genesis to Revelation
and every page in between.
Tribulation is a certainty,
death a guarantee,
only one solution for sinning man:
to your Saviour hasten flee.

So Yahweh freed His people,
lead them by cloud and fire
but despite many deliverances
Israel relied upon its own power.
Disobedient to The Almighty
they bowed to idol gold,
confined then to the wilderness,
forty years in sand abode.

Liberty again granted
under Joshua's command,
Yahweh remained faithful
as His tribes reached Promised Land,
then over many generations
leaders raised both good and bad,
periods of close allegiance
but at other times they fell.

Years of steady progress,
other decades away from home,
Assyria and Babylon,
control under empire Rome.
Titus came on his rampage,
the Temple he did burn,
judgement from The Highest
when His people refused to turn.

A Diaspora akin to Babel,
His children banished from His land,
their promised return millennia later
which occurred after satan's holocaust brand.
God's faithfulness stands in testimony,
to His Words of prophecy,
Israel, once more a nation,
then eternity.

It was now not this world
that had Hail Fellow despondent,
his meditations confirmed
he better here than leave this world dead.
Visions of devils at night encircled,
voices of demons alive in his head;
of hell he assured
but unprepared for the dread.

In a time of great stress
one yearns to find silence
for anxiousness and fear
strip confidence away,
numbing of insides,
crumbling intestines,
no clear thinking
as time drifts away.

Now that death stalked him
he clung vainly onto life,
clinging to scorched ground
with all struggle of desperate might,
trepidation and horror
became now his grim home
while he sought to hide,
to evade caskets sealed tomb.

Bang. Bang. Bang,
o'er the horizon,
the last judgements,
God's wrath on the earth,
those alive
quaking and shaking,
cursing their parents
for the day of their birth.

There were two peoples left
upon the face of earth,
those very few left of light
and those of shadow dark.
One group destined for glory
to worship at The Master's feet,
the others who took the mark,
they who worshiped the image of beast.

Those left alive had taken
full assault of brunt,
each vainly hoped an end,
unaware of coming hurt.
The Lord released His angel
despatched with bowl in hand,
and poured its contents out
emancipating loathsome sores on the skin of every man.

Sores upon the people
who accepted the beast's mark,
to those who had not repented,
who had beast worshipped from their hearts.
Like Egypt's sixth plague,
painful welts and sores,
pus filled red flared,
deep itch of flesh fresh gored.

No escape from this torment,
no salve of comforts oil,
fluids painful red skin,
growing, gnawing, vile.
Painful to the touch,
crescendo of echo roars,
no cure found for these men
who grew these loathsome sores.

City and troubled townland,
direction east and west,
The Lord's gift
to the children of the beast.
Townland and rural country,
positions north and south,
poisoned breath emitted
from sinful idolatrous hearts.
The second angel poured his bowl,
all the sea was destroyed,
akin the second trumpets scourge
salt seas were turned to blood.
It happened without warning,
no time to trawl for food,
all living creatures in the sea
died forevermore.

Thick, viscous, clogging,
like the circulation of a corpse,
earth's arteries of voyage
hardened solid like a crust,
a desert of disorder,
no flow from crimson tide,
Ichor of all false gods
brought to court and tried.

Guilty was their verdict
the earth heavy from fallen blood,
waiting for final sentence
allotted by eternal's Judge.
Shipping beached and red hulled,
stuck in blood sludge muck,
no escape for wayward crews
when judged by God above.

Hail Fellow watched the sea
as the waters turned to blood,
he no longer surprised
to witness judgements from above.
He stopped and shrugged his shoulders
and turned to walk at pace,
to find himself some fresh water
to fish and bathe sore face.

As he marched for a river
the third angel poured his bowl
and like the first plague of Egypt
fresh waters were assailed.
All rivers and springs of water
to blood their contents turned,
no water left on earth,
akin the flood, all flesh The Lord had spurned.

Noah had preached righteousness
over one hundred years he completed task,
under Yahweh's instruction
built an ark to save his clan.
He entered with his loved ones,
The Lord then closed the door,
then over and under the earth's crust
came the sound of torrents roar.

When the rains were over
The Lord promised His respite,
never again the earth to drown,
rainbows covenant still intact.
But just like the days of Noah
all flesh was found corrupt,
The Lord was preparing His kindling
for the ground to char and burn.

Blood is the price of ransom,
Blood; The Lord's anointed seal,
painted over Egypt's doorways,
His love to soon reveal.
Blood is the price of violence,
saint and prophet called His name,
blood became the judgement
for blood reveals all shame.

The fourth angel left Heaven
with bowl of heat in hand,
he cast it to the ground
to scorch every living man.
Temperatures had been rising,
unseasonal bake and boil
but now heat like no other
cast from judgements vial.

No waters left for succour,
the atmosphere dry and parched,
records at all highs
as if the globe would burst.
A cauldron of Sahara
each hemisphere endured,
those alive cursed God,
no repentance left; no cure.

Hail Fellow Merry recoiled,
his skin sand blast with heat,
dragged he his weakened frame
by hand and stretch of feet,
his head was fried and blistered,
enflamed his tongue in mouth,
he begged to die and wondered why
no end to anguish curse.

Then like a bolt of lightening
as fast as speed of light,
darkness enveloped the whole world,
the fifth angel's bowl attack.
Darkness from the heavens,
Egypt's ninth plague replayed,
but not confined by geography,
this time all regions were enslaved.

Men gnawed their tongues in darkness
in midst of heat and sores,
torment upon each human
for the beast they each had chose.
Still they screamed their blasphemy,
cursed Yahweh from their hearts,
no reprieve for sinning man,
no relief from pains or sores.

The sixth bowl purchased a two prong attack.
the first to dry the Euphrates,
the second, principalities and powers to attract.
The Euphrates a target,
pathway for the kings of the East,
while three unclean spirits like frogs,
loosed from the dragon,
the mouth of the beast.

The kings of the earth,
those graspers of power and temporal might,
were drawn by the unclean spirits
by lying signs and works of slight.
Hooks in their mouths,
all sense and reason those demons did deaden,
the kings drawn to The Almighty's battle,
called in Hebrew; Armageddon.

And so the world did meet its end
and like a winter blanket
Yahweh did the earth then fold,
exposing all unrighteousness, lies and works,
He terminated satan's timed leasehold.
Sovereign,
His last judgement to undertake,
the seventh bowl; the earth to shake.

The seventh angel poured his bowl into the air,
"It is done!" announced a voice from Heaven's throne,
an earthquake hit the earth and broke its bones,
an orchestra of thundering,
great lightening on patrol.
Out of kilter the earth began to sway,
mountains, islands vanished
this feared and fateful day.

Death's horror stalked in open sight that day,
out from under cover cutting people freely down,
the grim reaper piled his corpses reward high
and claimed his bounty vigourously by city and by town.
The great city fell into three parts
and every nation fell,
Babylon, The Harlot, was judged,
her sorcery extinguished at the peel of death's bell.

Appointed onto death once, to judgement we must go,
the idols we place our trust in all exposed.
Our fornications, adulteries, each our untempered lusts,
our treasures vain, our false gods all corrupted into rust.
Murders of the heart, our violent shed of blood,
ambitions to our selfish ends, The Lord to each will show.
Our pretensions, our flatteries, all our lies and sins,
even all the secrets, hidden from our life's begin.

Pummelled by hail,
great balls of ice weight ball,
those not recorded in The Book of Life,
sent to Hades and after judgement Hell.
A block of crooked chipped masonry,
fell upon his head,
thats how Hail Fellow Merry
became Hail Fellow Dead.

Part 5

Down the deep darkness

"I am He who lives and was dead,
and behold, I am alive forevermore. Amen.
And I have the keys of Hades and of Death."

(Rev. 1:18.)

DOWN THE DEEP DARKNESS

Dark is the shading,
dark,
the colour of the pit,
down the deep darkness,
black revealed in pitch.

Dark has no vague shadow,
dark,
walls invisible thick,
down the deep darkness,
black piled prison brick.

Dark is the sound of terror,
echoes,
fierce off bounce surround,
down the deep darkness,
black is grims death reward.

Dark is the conscience of dissention,
dark,
all hope forever impaired,
down the deep darkness,
demons sound alerts beware.

Dark the residence of hostile,
dark,
surrender of the mind,
down the deep darkness,
the earth's mirage you've left behind.

Twelve parts this body,
some as hard as bone,
male and female He created them,
DNA chromosomes.
Intricately they are built,
each fearfully made,
each system built;
tailor-made.

Internal framework
tough as nails,
housing wonders
and minds that think,
supporting movements
protecting parts weak,
accommodating vessels and lungs,
each one unique.

The nervous system
communicating thoughts,
learning and memory
each identifiable part,
neurons and atoms,
organs and cords,
cells constructing
around each nerve.

Muscular function
moving those bones
visceral muscles
help move the blood,
heartbeats rhythm
pumping life,
pushing childbirth's
babe to light.

Growing old they say
makes one wise,
legacy's lesson
afore one dies.
Joy and uncertainty,
pleasure and pain,
declining by aging,
obituary captures last date and name.

Built for God's glory
in His image each is made,
destined for Heaven
but by sin all pierced grace.
The spiritual dimension
most fail to recognise,
for from enmity's heart
Yahweh each despised.

By the wages of sin
the purchase of death,
the miracle of life
stopped short in breath,
systems collapsing,
blood slows in each vein,
heart beats then slower,
awaiting scythe's blade.

Oxygen is cut short
from brain and from lungs,
breathing erratic,
last gasps rattle bones.
Two days after passing
internal organs decompose,
then bloating and leaking
from mouth, end and nose.

Fifty years decomposes tissue,
eighty years for your bones,
ashes to ashes,
vain imaginations dethroned.
For each one a funeral,
for both saved and for lost,
then by the mourner's second drink
your memory is toast.

Each will die,
to all an end,
but where will you,
your eternity spend?
To die In Christ
is to be present with The Lord,
but to die condemned
His door is forever closed.

The rich man and Lazarus
both lived their lives,
connected by geography
in era's same time,
to Abraham's bosom
Lazarus did fly,
the rich man still awaits judgement
to this very day.

A deep pit now his home,
awaiting second death,
sentence at the very end
from Yahweh's rule and timely wrath,
destined for hell,
eternal's hot flame,
he knowing whats coming
still relives full his shame.

Thus so it was,
his tale we must tell,
awaiting in Hades
before plummet to hell,
Hail Fellow Dead,
full extract of reward,
down the deep darkness
where sin's torment is found.

Down the deep valley
from where no one ever steps back,
an encroaching tunnel,
abysmal in black,
this valley of death for Hail Fellow Dead,
twisting and turning,
limbs akimbo haphazard in flail,
contorting, grotesque shapes,
mis-shapen in dread.
No vision of light,
all exceedingly dull,
obsidian colour
his death mask unfurled,
cascading and falling like swirls autumn leaf,
winters approach,
his fate locked and sealed.
His body he left
as he stepped into black
but with every sensation
and auditory attack,
his last moments remembered
just before his last choke
as a grim hand clenched him
from black smokes dark abode.
His body he left
as the stepped out of the world,

a heightened awareness
as death shook its hold.
It seemed like forever
his fall to this place,
a collection of memories
etched, wrinkle stained his face,
terrifying darkness
this tunnel of flight,
he aware of a demon,
one on each side.
He started to scream
as loud as could voice
but no one could hear,
no last minute advice,
no name to call on,
no one to save,
destined for the pit
when he had hoped just for a grave.

His life his own masterpiece,
wild abandon in paint,
now a full realisation:
he had relinquished God's grace.

Next without warning,
a bleak cell with a thud,
velocity broken
with full stop jolt shock,
the speed of light force whittled away,
like a fall from a parachute
before landing on clay.
A pierce of skin howl,
full body recoil,
gut stench of blood rot,
emotions uncoiled.

Some scream forever,
some scream for a day,
some, this being their expectation
have nothing to say.
The first scream of terror
unleashed with intensity of voice,
sore, raw, numb throated
in which devils rejoice;
no matter how long one screams
the first pitch decibel is never replayed.
There is no rest for the unholy
from sins manifest hold,
locked,
isolated until judgement,
little seen but everything heard.
Emotions visit,
hopeless despair,
one would pull it all out
if one still had their hair!
For a time undetermined
Hail Fellow Dead revisited his past,
in life he desired no part of God,
today
The Almighty duly granted that wish.

Heat, scorch heat
in this bottomless pit,
perpetual time, cavern deep,
no respite,
no restful sleep,
no escape
from heat, scorch heat.

Arrayed in black his punished soul,
justices outpouring
under wrath's control,
attentive ears heighten fears vigilant guard
for demons roam in the prowling hour.
Taunting voices
with drag of chains,
numbing echoes
of his called name,
"Hail Fellow Merry
you're now Hail Fellow Dead,
soon to burn
in the heat scorch of hell."
Clinking and scratching these metallic sounds
while screams surround his prison walls,
voices of burden,
mouths foam spit,
sealed for judgement
in the bottomless pit.
Terror and clamour every hour,
no release from restitutions ire,
despotic creatures opening his door,
their quick withdraw,
voice's shout box hoarse,
throat screamed raw.

The stench of death attacked his frame,
a putrid hold of stink obscene,
the walls seemed wet
with drip sludge sick,
the cruel remains from previous heaves.
Then through the walls
visions grim,
pale green spectres
toward him they'd reach,
clawing and scraping like hungers grasp,

moving parts like sting rattle asps,
pummelling,
punching,
vomit bile,
Hail Fellow Dead all peace denied,
their quick disappear again through walls,
the prisoner collapsed
in his world of small.

The times of silence were desperate short,
no rest for the wicked
in the pitchest of dark,
his mind in chaos,
little emotion he'd feel,
his thoughts always scrambled
from demons pulverising zeal.

Sometimes the visit of a demon quiet,
just stand in the corner,
no sound of voice,
no screams or coil of chains,
just sly malevolence
in green skinned pale.
This was the worst for Hail Fellow Dead,
the silence of suffering,
chaotic fear of hidden dread.

In the brief moments of silence
lurks the weary truth,
this is forever,
eternal,
no hope.
Each time the silence came
he relived that thought,
this is eternal,
its each revelation panicked as the first.

This is the first time
Hail Fellow Dead,
forever, eternal
to live midst the dead;
no expectation of punishments relent,
no opportunity left to ever repent.

Sometime later
he could not discern when
for time stands still
past the earth's violent end,
maybe a year,
perhaps more,
a faint sound penetrated
his prison cell door.

thump.

thump.

thump.

At first so faint,
growing louder
with furious pace,
THUMP, THUMP, THUMP,
with metal spear grind,
a troop,
a legion,
stopped outside,
his door squealed open like a farmyard barn,
emitted a noise,
a forewarn of harm.
To a dark corner Hail Fellow fled
for there is nothing good to look forward to
in the residence of dead.

A silhouette dressed in mercenary black,
buttons, insignia and pointed hat,
a chief it seemed
of prison guard,
skeletal frame,
cruel look so hard,
a finger pointed, crooked bone of white
beckoned Hail Fellow to follow,
marshalled tight,
a long walk midst stench of fiends,
no talk,
not a whisper,
no information he gleaned.
This parade
designed to shock,
to further frighten the host of lost,
to quench any little remaining hope.

At last a door frame,
huge vacant hall,
a pew placed
to kneel at a throne.
Satan himself entered and sat,
extending his ring
for Hail Fellow to clasp
and sitting observing Hail Fellow at kneel,
the devil opened his mouth
and began his long speech.

"I am the beginning of this your end,
baptised into turmoil
I am the king of the world,
it is I now, you're regal,
whom you'll forever serve.
I am the god of the deliberately lost,

no entry requirement,
no bloody cross,
no reliance on miracles
just distortion and lies,
I am murder's father,
the thief of the night.
Stepped I into Eden at the very first,
coil of a serpent,
barer of curse,
tempted the woman with the taste of unknown,
deceived her husband,
their God's plan was blown.
They were cast out of the garden to my wholesome rejoice,
having extracted knowledge of evil
to shape their free choice.
I baited the brothers,
soaked one in his blood,
mayhem and madness
survived even the flood.
I was created in Majesty; Lucifer bright,
I knew I could better
His works by my slight,
launched out to this world
I brought angels third
and built my own kingdom
His plans to usurp.

I thwarted his workings,
I poured out my scorn,
Egypt,
then Babylon,
ruinous Rome,
empires and armies my wars they did rage
the best of my works captured on history's page.

I raised up my leaders
to name but a few,
Pharaoh, Jezebel, Caesars not few,
Nebuchadnezzar from Babylon
I charted his course
and levelled Yahweh's city,
by the thousands shed blood.

A seed had been promised
to Abraham of old,
by generations passing
I kept my observe,
plotted and schemed
I maimed and I pillaged,
awaiting His Saviour
I vowed I would kill.
I punished, I trod,
so many destroyed,
at long last His Babe,
I quick ended His voice.
I had invented crucifixion,
death by sharp nail,
body to hang
at Rome's cruel impale.
Jesus was captured,
His body I flayed
and casting by lots
my ejection I repaid.
Jesus Christ died
though some say He arose,
I disregarded this herald,
my choice to ignore.
I continued to ravage,
I continued to kill,
enjoyed me my murders

and the blood they would spill.
I hold no regard for humans,
spared life no second thought,
delicate their anatomy,
resilient
but fragile to knocks;
their battered bruised lives
through which I extracted falsehoods hurt.

I am the author of confusion,
by strength of illusion
I established their thrones.
cultures and traditions
I led to the slaughter
and by concocting wars reasons
I brought millions here home.
Invented I false gods,
strongholds of emotion,
demagogues demanding sacrifice
to idols of stone.
I was the plotter,
violent deposer,
the dreamer of wicked nefarious schemes,
leading all blindly, in circles they'd follow,
unknowingly worshipping
tribal anthems extreme.

My wars and my leaders,
blood thirsty connivers,
from ancient of days
these demons I'd raise,
wars and rumours
down through the ages;
herein my short summary
at every stage.

Egypt my pride,
Pharaohs installed,
whipped they the Hebrews
to eradicate Holy call.
Assyria, Babylon, their magnificent palaces,
Medes and Persia
God's people enslaved.
Sparta's brave warriors,
children handed over
I trained them to kill,
wars constructed, potentates to raze.
Later the Scythians,
dark suits of armour,
I unleashed them to slaughter,
death by long blade.
Arose I the Greeks,
young Alexander,
I killed him in short life
all the world he did conquer,
then raised up Rome,
savouring preparations, Son Christ to erase.
Rome's Punic wars,
Germania and Gaul,
Caesars to court
and their triumph parades,
then my friend Nero,
killed he the Christians,
Rome set on fire,
he found someone to blame.

I killed his disciples,
His message endangered,
continued my plotting
with seditious intent,
I moved my eyes worldwide,

India, China,
the Huns, the Goths
my vision they plied.
In each little corner
I deposited my leaning,
installing my minions,
my agenda their wage,
I founded institutions,
governments in tandem,
ruled I all lands,
I lord of the seas.

The Middle East became my focus,
the battleground of nomads I fought to protect,
if I could stop the Lords full anointing
forever it seemed,
His land I would keep.
The Arabian Gulf and all land surrounding,
ruled I the deserts,
the ports of the waves,
the Spanish, then Charlemagne,
Lombard's and Saxons,
Viking and Normans,
my pleasure their waste;
all these great peoples
for a time I short raised.
Then in the midst,
England's great empire,
a jewel in my crown
I started to build.

Rebuilding requires devious attack,
Urban's crusades ordained Jerusalem's sack,
later Thomas Becket was killed,
dared he to venture Christ's church status first before my king
and when Minamoto Yoritomo, the first Shogun

took my Supreme Commander title
I just had to strike him down.
I revived an old word,
placed its hate on violent hearts:
heretic,
and many righteous I burnt off earth's crust.
The Mongols I raised,
Xanadu's Kublai Khan
and I stalked the globe with
black death's spawn.
Imagine a war of one hundred years,
Agincourt where fifth Henry
directed his arrows to harm.
The world's moments of merriment
I conceived to ruin,
renaissance, exploration and fine printed page;
my choicest ambition,
wars fought over God;
I gloried and revelled when love disappeared.
Mercator's world maps I used for my plans,
early thoughts visited on how men I could brand,
Pilgrims to America where many took flight,
I destroyed over centuries through inside attack.

Descartes,
I think, therefore I am,
distilled to my take,
you think thoughts that I shape!

Pirates and Cossacks,
Frederick the Great,
Industrial revolution prophesised demise of man's fate,
factories and chimneys,
pits for the coal,
millions of mere children
fuelled the mills under my avarice hold.

Revolutions built empires,
Napoleon,
Waterloo,
guillotine executions as fraternity grew,
steam trains, slave trades,
opium wars,
the whole cosmos engineered
toward two horrific world wars.
Mechanisation swept in to kill,
bullets of speed cutting down all who fell,
motorised mayhem by tank blast shell,
ushering the unwitting; destination my hell.

In quiet observation,
secluded in the armoury
I did my best work
twisting and forging the inventions of men,
channelling funding
for dystopia's churning
all that was made for good
I conformed to my will.

The rise of antichrists,
Haman's spirit reliving to kill all the Jews,
segregation, apartheid,
all played their role;
transhuman agendas,
my unholy trinity,
nuclear oblivion took the last toll.

I've felt with satisfaction,
the reward of distraction,
the whole wide world
is just a history of war......

Hail Fellow, I admired you're defiance,
it made me think of alliance,
my legion of evil
I thought you might join.
A uniform of pure wicked,
epaulettes for your shoulders,
you'd do my bidding
in my temple of doom.

What do you say Hail Fellow Dead?
Have you succumbed,
succumbed to my charm?"

Hail Fellow looked,
his eyes craftily narrowed,
etch of a smile
cruel tainted his mouth.

But all of a sudden
he felt the ground open,
he found himself standing before Jesus;
his second death loomed.

Part 6

Down the deep burning

"And behold, I am coming quickly,
and My reward is with Me,
to give to everyone according to his work.

I am the Alpha and the Omega,
the Beginning and the End,
the First and the Last."

(Rev. 22:12-13.)

DOWN THE DEEP BURNING

Shut out the screams
you'll hear the fire,
thumping heart heat
of tempest cage,
devouring,
scouring,
white scorch blast.
Melting,
churning,
down deep flash.

Close your eyes,
hear burns sound,
crackle stick snap
smokes surround,
thick and poisonous
noxious trail,
vicious fumes,
deaths impale.

Glowing bodies ember bright,
cadaver torches,
sinners plight.
No escape from devil's hell,
hear the sounds,
smell the smell.

Hail Fellow Dead bowed his knee
as every mortal will,
then shepherded, shielded by The Saviour
was brought to summit hill,
vast stretch of eternity's horizon,
all span of history's time,
Hail Fellow acknowledged in wonder,
all chaos left behind.

Christ pointed to the devil
that menace twist of old
and squirming, worming forward
satan knew his time had come.
Then pointed Jesus,
the grim shadow tried to plead,
then pointed Jesus
and satan bowed to kneel.

"Observe now sinful Hail Fellow,
behold your mighty king,
you trusted in a vanity,
see soon the reward it brings.
We need not Ourselves justify
for there is no dark in truth,
observe now satan's judgement,"
at the devil Christ did not even look.

"His pride desired,
he craved a bigger world,
so We gave him his doom,
We acceded to his choice.
We cast that heathen out,
like lightening o'er ground sparse
he and his henchmen,
We cast the devil out.

He boasted,
he betrayed the fidelity,
the fiefdom of Our dominion
to parade on fallen earth,
he exchanged eternity,
all wholesome, all love,
he exchanged The Father's expressed desire
for an empty purse of false.

The charge is sin against all that is Holy.
The charge, blasphemy against Our Name.
The charge, idolatry and subsequent religious cheating.
The charge, murderous malevolent defame.
The charge, sedition and unlawful treason.
The charge, wars and scheme of malicious intent.
The charge, shedding of innocent blood,
The charge, birthing the earth it's death.

As he knows there is no trial in Heaven,
just a verdict right and true,
by grace one is either under My blood
or the statement – you I never knew.
Guilty therefore is this satan.
Guilty therefore this king of lies.
Guilty his preserve of pride and boasting.
Guilty therefore his idolatrous despise."

Christ's children had waited patiently,
for millennia they had held their claim,
patience had waned then God's promise remembered,
all understood that Yahweh would have His day.
A roar of thunderous cheer was mustered,
vengeance, justice, God's alone to pay,
Heaven now satisfied with the verdict
they stood back to witness satan's doomsday.

Hell had been prepared for the devil and his demons,
for the unholy and unrighteous;
doom.
Fire and brimstone,
torments cauldron,
damnation eternal; far removed.
Down the deep burning, down the deep burning,
down the deep burning the devil flew.

Behold next the false prophet,
crozier and mitre tidy in place,
"See," he declared, "Lord, I have delivered you a kingdom,
of my works and not by grace.
From my city of seven hilltops,
the world I swore for you I'd save,
drunk on my fornications
many heretics sent to forgotten graves.

Mystery Babylon the Great, the Mother of Harlots
and of the abominations of the earth,
is written bold upon my forehead,
I draped in gold and pearls.
All of the worlds fortunes
I bestow to you this day,
all brought under my dominion,
every king and government brought craftily under my sway."

"Behold! Your Babylon is fallen,"
announced Christ Jesus in reply.
"I AM the Creator and Saviour,
grace is not of man but gifted through Our second birth."
Fire and brimstone, torments cauldron,
damnation eternal; far removed.
Down the deep burning, down the deep burning,
down the deep burning the false prophet flew.

Next the petrified demons,
each trembling alone, trying best to hide,
from creations first dawning
fallen spirits had picked the wrong side.
They roared,
they screamed in anguish,
their slaughter soon each knew,
despatched forever to eternals fire damned stew.

Hideous contortions,
gnashing teeth and spit,
these despoilers of earth found guilty,
to fall like swine from summit cliff.
Fire and brimstone, torments cauldron,
damnation eternal; far removed.
Down the deep burning, down the deep burning,
down the deep burning every last rotten demon flew.

"Come Hail Fellow with Me to observe
for the world of evil I will purge,
every sinister element I must sack,
those of murderous fork-tongued attack."
With no flourish of His mighty hand
The Lord summoned that awful band,
a door opened, they shuffled forth,
eyes cast downward for each was damned.

First out Revelations purveyors of death,
leaders of desperate battle charge,
against The Lord they had taken stand,
each now anticipating their judgement's demand.
Gog of Magog, Meshech and Tubal,
Gomer, Togarmah, Libya too,
at the rear Ethiopia and Persia,
of their impending doom each vagabond knew.

"Israel is Our jewel,
the apple of Our eye,
all history of scripture
you cannot deny.
From Babel's dispersion
to very end of days
Our prophets announced
that We would have Our say.

You desired Israel's requiem,
you readied your orchestra, violins and bows,
yet by Our hand by hail
your armies strong We did dispose."
Fire and brimstone, torments cauldron,
damnation eternal; far removed.
Down the deep burning, down the deep burning,
down the deep burning Revelation's criminals flew.

Next the unholy trinity
as outlined in Isaiah fourteen,
all the chief ones of the earth
He had raised up to their thrones,
the kings of the nations
sent He their pomp down to Sheol;
the maggot was spread
over secrets untold.

Brewers of concoctions in shiny bright vials,
their own Bunsen burners
He set to destroy,
kindle ignited for hells sombre flame.
Despotic corporate leaders,
they of exaggerated stock, manipulators of price,
Christ Jesus' formulation;
their death suffered twice.

Then blind leaders of the blind
in a long studious line,
all the knowledge of the world in head
but beating hearts rhythm stone cold dead.
Fire and brimstone, torments cauldron,
damnation eternal; far removed.
Down the deep burning, down the deep burning,
down the deep burning the unholy trinity flew.

Then those of history past
He called each out by name,
leaders, emperors,
kings of stately mane,
politicians, generals,
celebrities, ego vain,
ushered in and judged
under Sovereign's throne of grace.

Arrogance and pride
had been their means of grace,
embossed on coin of realm,
each stamped their own full face,
empty shills conformed
to the image of temporal whim,
God had been calling each one
each day from their begin.

Next the heaving masses,
millions lined and stooped,
the longest line ever recorded
those not written in Lamb's book.
All outside of Christ's shed blood
arraigned for court's verdict,
those whose sins had not been forgiven,
those marked by six, six, six.

Feared they all the dark of night
when all around in perished plight
feigned reliance on false idol of man's cut stone.
No Light beyond in yonder flame,
no truth bearer, no saving Name,
no lantern to beckon warm cast of home's bright gold.
At last sentence fell, all to smother,
committing them, young and old, all to eternals suffer.

Repent. Repent.
each had heard but each had also spurned,
now all too late
for the hour of life had for each already turned.
Fire and brimstone, torments cauldron,
damnation eternal; far removed.
Down the deep burning, down the deep burning,
down the deep burning every unrepentant sinner flew.

Hell was nearly full,
just room for one unfortunate more,
Hail Fellow slowly turned
from the lake that burns with fire,
he bowed his knees
surveyed all from above,
and considered The Judge not robed in black
but clothed and dressed in love.

At the last his brain wheel turned,
Hail Fellow understood,
the full authority of redeeming grace;
Christ's full measure of saving love.
This Jesus, Hail Fellow had rejected,
this Jesus he had despised,
now Christ stood in power resurrected
with compassion in His eyes.

Jesus Christ, The Word of God,
victorious over death,
sitting on a white horse
bright robe bloodied, dipped in red.
He who is faithful and true,
eyes like flame of fire,
the wearer of all heavenly crowns
full weight of Majesty's power.

Unto the world the child born
He had become a King,
Judge, Lord, High Priest eternal,
Everlasting Father and Prince of Peace.
Upon the throne of David,
established forever more,
His judgement and justice to reign supreme,
King of Kings and Lord of Lords.

Anointed over all living,
anointed over all dead,
anointed High Priest over Melchizedek,
Redeemer of sinful men by grace.
Opener of the seals,
all history His command,
The Sovereign of salvation
and every work by hand.

He took the frame of weakness,
He perished through cruel death,
resurrected upon the third day,
He served His Father's will.
Silent afore the shearer,
Hail Fellow's time was soon,
offered freely life eternal
instead he chose his doom.

Alleluia to He risen,
Lord of love and life,
Alleluia to God's anointed,
Defeater of Calvary's plight.
Praise Him who lives forever,
praise Him forever more,
yesterday, today and tomorrow,
praise Christ Jesus the Shepherd of the Door.

The Lord Jesus bid Hail Fellow,
they turned, observed to north,
Hail Fellow was offered a faint glimpse
as Heaven beckoned forth,
visions dulled like glass opaque
the old world suddenly dissolved,
passed away forever,
a sleuth's mystery finally solved.

Behold, yonder horizon,
a new Heaven, a new earth
resided in by those repentant
by grace those gifted Christ's new birth.
Jesus pointed to His new city
coming down from God,
New Jerusalem, Alleluia,
prepared bride for husband Lord.

The tabernacle of God
to dwell with redeemed men,
He in their midst
He the temple; eternal Immanuel.
No more tears, no more death,
no sorrow, crying, pain,
all former things had passed away,
not brought to mind again.

Jesus Christ makes all things new,
He the Beginning and the End,
the fountain of life's waters running freely,
fully God and fully man.
All nations, tongues and peoples served,
multitudes to worship sing,
on their foreheads each His printed name,
reserved not for beast but King.
In the midst the Holy city
stood His tree of life,
all glory and honour given to God,
the New Jerusalem bathed in Light.
Stones of finest cutting,
Jasper, Sapphire bright,
Beryl, Topaz, Amethyst,
glint in crystal light.

Shape of square and flat as tall,
each side fifteen hundred miles,
north, south, east and west
twelve gates named for Israel's tribes.
Twelve angels stood, one each gate,
twelve foundations secured by The Rock,
home to all those by free grace given
new life in Lamb's life book.

Sorrows salt tear was shed by Fellow,
rolled down to chin then fell to breast,
no new life for misery's Hail Fellow,
a wasted life, full tinge regret.
This return to Eden, perfect, spotless,
only the forgiven to walk the halls,
those trusting in the Seed promised,
Genesis' beginning; Yahweh's promise born.

The first earth birthed at creation,
every breathing beast and leaf of green,
then rest of Sabbath upon completion,
measured realm; dimensions seen.
Clockwork plotted orchestrations,
thread of generations to begotten Son,
all authority throughout all ages,
every heartbeat, all living blood.

Throughout the years of battle wages,
the rage of men by war's unfold,
God Himself crucified on cursed ground mortal,
bled on soil, His blood dirt soaked.
Prophets, Kings announced His coming,
His promised return they identified,
the age of church, gentile salvation,
for Messiah an unblemished bride.

His focus Israel for Daniel's last seven,
144,000 servants He anointed by name,
announcing heavens eternal bounty,
Christ Jesus Messiah known now by name.
All by grace,
unmerited favour,
all by grace,
works not of man.

"Come Hail Fellow,"
The Lord quiet beckoned,
"Alas young man
thine judgement hour,
alas thou spurned sincerest calling,
thine fate now sealed beyond Our power.
There is no reasoning left, no succour,
thine sins stain crimson; forevermore."

"You are The Lord, but I was my own god,
I plied my time with ease of joy,
followed my nose,
erred to its leaning,
my conscience seared.
I craved my way.
I led myself into bondage,
my own impulse became my grave."

Hail Fellow stopped and deeply pondered,
ten commands of law his heart to slay.
"I carved my image of self importance,
arrogance of heart my badge of pride,
I yearned all to bow
at sound my name,
all above and earth beneath,
I sought advantage; their image to sway.

Your name I scorned,
despised all Holy,
Your Spirit I fled,
erased from brain,
I cursed and spat
at Your recollection,
anathema to me
Thine precious Name.

The Sabbath became a day of folly,
a restless, ceaseless, heaving day,
hedonistic rampage, brewed madness,
seeking flesh to forge my play.
I hallowed myself,
vain course I plotted,
seeking innocents
to lead astray.

My father, my mother,
I can't remember,
I didn't visit
for many years.
Always an excuse
found at the ready,
I preferred levity's riot
amongst my peers.

The opening of seals
facilitated blackness,
darkness of mind
etched my path,
many murders I deliberately committed,
mothers, children, their food to grasp.
I felt no guilt their breath I ending,
bloodlust hatred engorged my mind.

I embraced adultery
with ease of beckon,
a ladies' man
I'm proud to say,
many marriages I assassinated,
temptations lust would find a way,
cared not their hearts, just sought their bodies,
pursuing pleasure every day.

"You shall not steal,"
I scoffed on hearing,
my middle name "vice"
any opportunity for gain.
Smooth words I forged
to seek plunder's flutter,
I accumulated wealth
by stealth sought prize.

False witness I gave
with no blush redness,
few true words
have passed these lips,
I a paid mercenary
for tongues bought wages,
many foolish bystanders
I inveigled to trap.

What didn't I covet
upon the earth?
Nothing escaped
my lust or crave.
Wives, chattel, all bounty pleasure,
these are the memories I proudly parade.
I, Lord, became the centre,
I coveted all to secure false gain.

So there it is Lord if I'm not mistaken,
forgive if I missed any spree of crime,
I look back at a litany of suffering
deserving Your justice for all my lying.
I am a lost cause,
I cast my lot in deceptions name,
honestly if I could live life once more,
I know my heart, I'd do the same."

The Lord stood back to observe Hail Fellow,
no words left for the sinner to say.
"To your credit you are not pleading,
a more earnest sinner I've not met this day,
you know Hail Fellow, had you repented
your free release would by My grace have been paid
for I AM the life, the truth,
there was in the end no other way.

In the old world Love came calling,
I knew men's hearts but still I came,
in Me there was no condemnation,
My Father's will was My Name to save.
My blood cleanses all from sin,
took all your punishment
and hell's retribution,
penalty paid in full on Calvary's hill.

Pounded nails for man's dissention,
crown of thorn upon My head,
spat on, punched,
cruel stick beaten,
the brand of chastisement
I left to hang.
Finally rejected by My Father
for He saw sins distortion upon My frame.

Three days later I was resurrected,
presented Myself alive, many witnesses I saw,
the laws curse and all disobedience
paid for those believing in atonement's blood.
Is God unjust now who inflicts wrath?
How then justice? Which must be paid,
grace by love to those repentant,
eternal punishment for those not saved."

"Please Lord......
No......
Not hell!
Not flame forevermore!
Not eternal separation,
not gnashing of teeth and pain full sore!"

Justice's sentence brought a howl of wailed lament
for Hail Fellow Dead had rejected The Lord's free grace repent.

"My Word says there is none righteous,
none deserving, no: not one!
Guilty in failing one Holy law
that person is guilty of breaking all.
That is why I came to die,
Hail Fellow had you been on earth alone
I would still have in Love's Name come."
Christ Jesus turned His back; Hail Fellow fell from view.

Hail Fellow was cast to flame,
flailed tunnel by leg and arm,
those in hell, already there,
reached out to clasp and harm.
Abject oblivion would too have a bride,
Hail Fellow Dead by name,
the hell of no ending is Justice's reckon,
Hail Fellow to writhe in furnace flame.

Down the deep burning.
Down the deep burning.
Down the deep burning
Hail Fellow flew.
Fire and brimstone, torments cauldron,
damnation eternal; far removed.
Down the deep burning, down the deep burning,
down the deep burning Hail Fellow flew.

Down the deep burning,
Hail Fellow flew.

Epilogue

"He who testifies to these things says,
"Surely I am coming quickly."
Amen. Even so, come, Lord Jesus!

The grace of our Lord Jesus Christ
be with you all. Amen."

(Rev. 22:20-21.)

EPILOGUE ONE

TO BE SUNG AS A PSALMIST

God Incarnate He came to the earth,
God Incarnate He came to the earth,
To die for our sin,
To die for our sin,
God Incarnate He came to the earth.

He died on a broken tree,
The Lord took sin's curse for me,
That I trust in His Name,
Trust in His Name,
Christ Jesus died on a broken tree.

On the third day He rose from the dead,
On the third day He rose from the dead,
Let the heavens declare,
The earth rise to cheer,
On the third day Jesus rose from the dead.

Alleluia to God's Heavenly King,
Alleluia to God's only Son,
At His Father's right hand,
His father's right hand,
Alleluia to God's only son.

He came to give His children new life,
He came to give His children new life,
The Holy Spirit inside,
In me He doth reside,
He came to give His children new life.

And at the end of our day,
And at the end of our day,
That I will trust in His Name,
Jesus Christ's Name,
That I trust in His Holy Name.

EPILOGUE TWO

Through punished howl of scream and shudder
panic set in with seismic recoil,
Hail Fellow Dead, arms and legs flailing
disappeared into a vastness of eternal turmoil.
With a stretched scream of descending madness,
his vision blurred by speed of fall,
senses awakened, he fully conscious,
aware suddenly of familiar surround.

Some vague recognition, a degree of comfort,
bathed in sweat his head laid down,
thoughts discombobulated, heart beat pounding,
Hail Fellow found himself at home!
What a stunning realisation,
this dark dread journey had been a dream,
awake now, he pinched skin for feeling,
immersered face in water; alive it seemed.

Hail Fellow considered the mirror
where he had once been embarrassed red,
he revisited that foreboding memory
every detail relived in dread.
Events remembered, nauseous his stomach,
full knowledge in tears his sins unsealed,
aware now of his unholy depravity,
his conscience brought low by shame revealed.

"But The Lord is alive!"
Hail Fellow rejoiced,
"my sins He died for,
to Him I must turn.
I'll visit the preacher,

he that I scoffed at,
to explain my experience
and of Christ I might learn."

So off he journeyed
with a spring step so joyous,
his heart leapt inside him,
praise overflowed,
the preacher welcomed
with fellowship fervour,
the two sat together
to discuss the great dream.

The preacher too a forgiven sinner
he sat and listened,
examined the tale,
he understood The Lord's Holy Scripture,
Revelation's nuances,
he traced each stage.
Seals, trumpets, bowls and judgement,
each step confirmed; minutia's detail.

Considered response is always advantageous,
the talk subsided, they both bowed to pray,
then with mounting anticipation
the preacher considered what best to say.
"Hail Fellow I'm convinced The Lord is you calling,
a choice you've been gifted, you alone have to choose,
firstly to repent for your sins to be forgiven
or continue in a lifestyle where ultimately you lose."

He pulled no punches this holy warrior,
he outlined the reward of lies and deceit,
death of flesh and eternal punishment,
if Calvary denied: destruction complete.

"Yes hell is eternal but so too is Heaven,
so focus fully on why The Lord came,
His sacrifice for full atonement,
salvation purchased in His Holy Name."
Hail Fellow listened and quietly pondered,
each point resonated, he understood,
he stood back and politely questioned,
"answer me simply: what did The Lord do?"
"The Creator," in reply, "He came here to live,
to forgive our sins, He came to save,
the sinful cannot achieve this work of Yahweh,
for full forgiveness is a gift of God's grace.

One cannot pay coinage for salvation,
it is neither by works for we would boast,
only by the shedding of Blood comes salvation
and not by the blood of bull calf or goat.
The Lord Jesus stood out of Majesty,
took upon Himself our frail domain,
God incarnate ministered midst His people,
paid our ransom by death nail impale.

A cross was the sentence, He judged by the sinful,
crucifixion by Rome was Pilate's decree,
but Christ was innocent of all the charges,
my sins and yours pounded those nails.
Jesus was buried, friends entombed His body,
three days later He was resurrected alive,
after witnessing days He to Heaven ascended
and sits now secure at The Father's right side.

God's law is perfect, it is His Holy standard,
but however long we try, His law we can't keep,
Christ came to live a life sinless,
He upheld each point fully and stood in our place.

The penalty for law breaking is curse and damnation,
The Lord Jesus took that punishment for me,
He bore my sin upon His innocent shoulders
and credited by grace His righteousness to me.

What great love expressed by our Saviour,
leaving Heaven to come here for me,
He promised His Spirit to those who follow,
given at Pentecost and now to all who believe.
God The Holy Spirit teaching and prompting,
demonstrating righteousness and judgement to come,
convicting of sins and drawing to repentance,
all by grace freely by God's only Son."

"So only God Himself can forgive sins,"
this truth Hail Fellow exclaimed.
"My choice now is to repent and obediently follow
or cast continued derision upon His Name."

Hail Fellow chose free grace redemption,
he asked forgiveness for all of his sins,
The Lord ever faithful granted His pardon
Hail fellow repented by grace through faith.

Alleluia sang the angels
a sinner forgiven, one more home,
God's children took delight in Heaven
and sang thanksgiving praises at the foot of Christ's throne.

Hail Fellow rose slowly to leave the meeting,
a new creation in Christ about to leave,
he apologised again for years of sly scoffing,
the preacher forgave him; their relationship at ease.

"Listen Hail Fellow, free grace is not a licence,
remember the price that The Lord paid for thee,
take not this lightly but The Holy Spirit will guide you
and when you sin repent on your knees.

Many paths lead to eternal damnation,
only one to life; Christ Jesus the way.
Hail Fellow Merry you became Hail Fellow Dead
and that Hail Fellow Dead is now Hail Fellow Saved."
He turned and nodded this Hail Fellow Saved,
knew in his heart it all of God's grace,
in a fountain of tears with voice near choking
he leaned toward the preacher and these final words spoke.

"My friend, I've been thinking," his words stumbled slowly,
"What a blessing this day I freely received...

It is there, you know... in the midst of all chaos...

In the midst of dystopia... by God's grace lives HOPE!"

* * *

Now dear reader, this is our journey,
the events described will soon unfold.

I ask you to think and carefully ponder;
what or who are you trusting in
and where is your HOPE?

"IT IS FINISHED"

Other books by Redmond Holt

Testimony: Onward toward salvation.

Mammon

Eulogy: Jerusalem 70AD.

America

Are you inspired to write a book?

Contact

Maurice Wylie Media
Your Inspirational & Christian Book Publisher
Based in Northern Ireland, serving readers worldwide

www.MauriceWylieMedia.com

www.ingramcontent.com/pod-product-compliance
Lightning Source LLC
Chambersburg PA
CBHW041144110526
44590CB00027B/4124
* 9 7 8 1 9 1 5 2 2 3 3 6 4 *